Bilingual Picture Dictionaries

My First Book of
Hindi
Words

by Katy R. Kudela

Translator: Translations.com

apple
सेब
(seb)

raintree
– publishers for children

Contents

How to use this dictionary

This book is full of useful words in both Hindi and English. The English word appears first, followed by the Hindi word. Look below each Hindi word for help to sound it out. Try reading the words aloud.

Topic heading in English

Topic heading in Hindi

Word in English
Word in Hindi
(pronunciation)

English: **body**

Hindi: शरीर (SHA-rir)

hair
बाल
(BA-l)

head
सिर
(sir)

ear
कान
(KA-n)

eye
आँख
(AA-nkh)

nose
नाक
(NA-k)

mouth
मुँह
(mu-ha)

arm
भुजा
(bhu-ja)

hand
हाथ
(HA-th)

leg
पैर
(pair)

foot
पाँव
(PA-nv)

6

7

Notes about the Hindi language

Hindi is written in the Devanagari alphabet and draws vocabulary from Sanskrit. Hindi has 14 vowels and 33 consonants.

Devanagari is written from left to right, but capital letters are not used.

The Hindi language easily adopts foreign words. English words like "car," "bus" and "computer" are written in Devanagari script but are pronounced like English.

In Hindi, the number six is pronounced (chhah). The extra "h" means the "ch" sound should be pronounced while breathing out heavily.

In Hindi, some words have no emphasis placed on syllables. These pronunciations are shown without capital letters.

3

uncle
चाचा
(CHA-cha)

mother
माता
(MA-ta)

cousin
चचेरे भाई-बहन
(cha-chere BHAI-ba-hen)

aunt
चाची
(CHA-chi)

baby
बच्चा
(ba-CHCHA)

grandmother
दादी
(DA-di)

father
पिता
(pi-ta)

grandfather
दादा
(DA-da)

brother
भाई
(BHAI)

sister
बहन
(ba-hen)

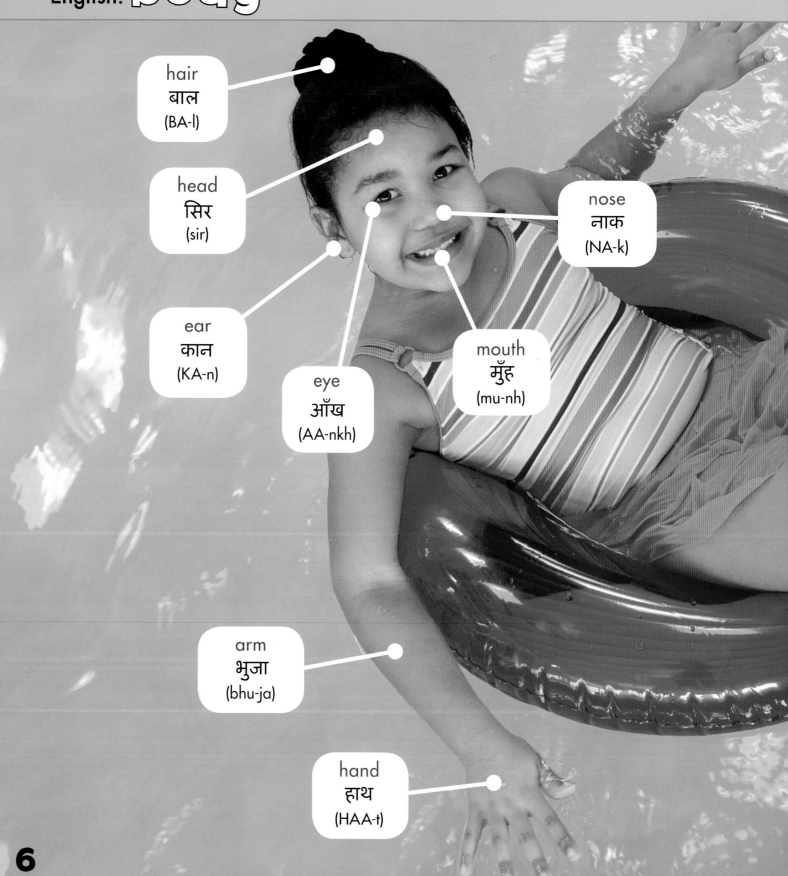

hair
बाल
(BA-l)

head
सिर
(sir)

ear
कान
(KA-n)

eye
आँख
(AA-nkh)

nose
नाक
(NA-k)

mouth
मुँह
(mu-nh)

arm
भुजा
(bhu-ja)

hand
हाथ
(HAA-t)

leg
पैर
(pair)

foot
पाँव
(PA-nv)

pyjamas
पजामा
(pa-JA-MA)

coat
कोट
(KOHT)

shorts
शॉर्ट्स
(shorts)

boot
बूट
(boot)

8

shoe
जूता
(joo-TA)

hat
टोपा
(TO-pa)

trousers
पैंट
(pants)

sock
मौज़ा
(MAU-za)

dress
पोशाक
(po-SHA-k)

shirt
शर्ट
(SHURT)

kite
पतंग
(pa-tang)

doll
गुड़िया
(gu-di-YA)

puzzle
पहेली
(pa-he-li)

train
ट्रेन
(trane)

wagon
वैगन
(vai-gan)

puppet
कठपुतली
(kart-pu-ta-lee)

skateboard
स्केटबोर्ड
(SKATE-bord)

skipping rope
कूदने वाली रस्सी
(koo-dane VA-LI ras-si)

ball
बॉल
(bawl)

bat
बैट
(bat)

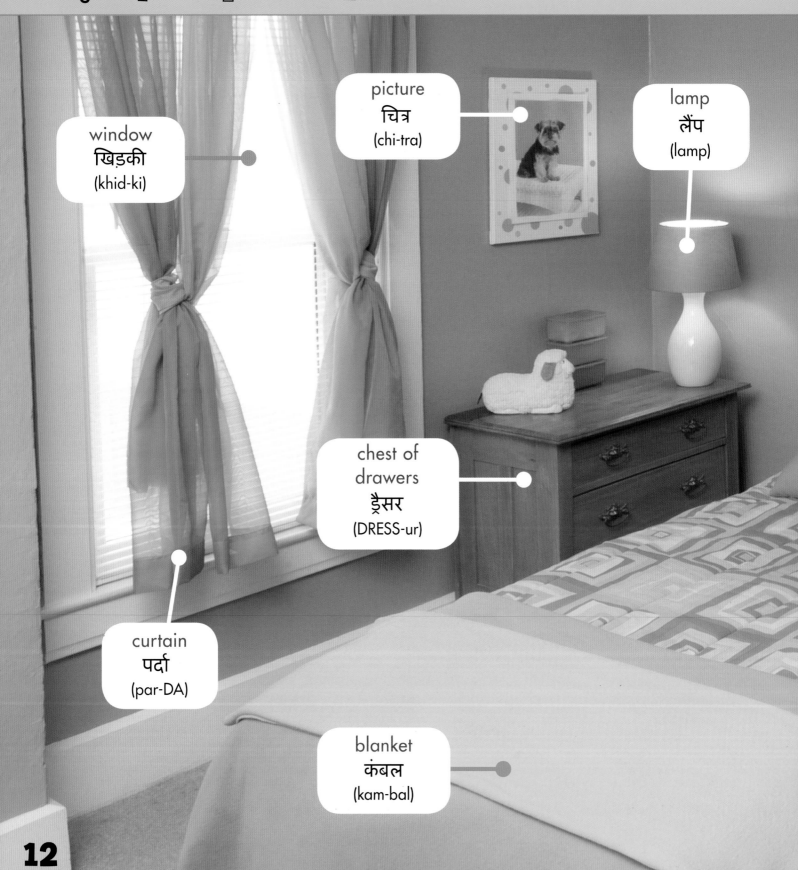

picture
चित्र
(chi-tra)

lamp
लैंप
(lamp)

window
खिड़की
(khid-ki)

chest of
drawers
ड्रैसर
(DRESS-ur)

curtain
पर्दा
(par-DA)

blanket
कंबल
(kam-bal)

12

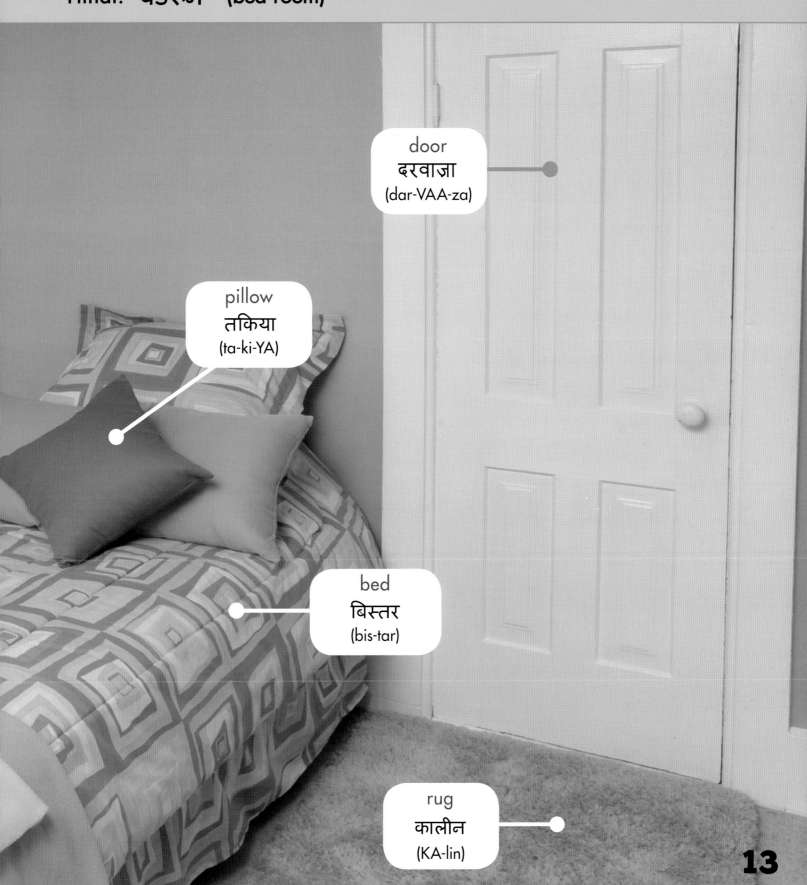

door
दरवाज़ा
(dar-VAA-za)

pillow
तकिया
(ta-ki-YA)

bed
बिस्तर
(bis-tar)

rug
कालीन
(KA-lin)

13

bath
बाथटब
(BATH-tuhb)

soap
साबुन
(SAA-bune)

toilet
टॉयलेट
(TOI-let)

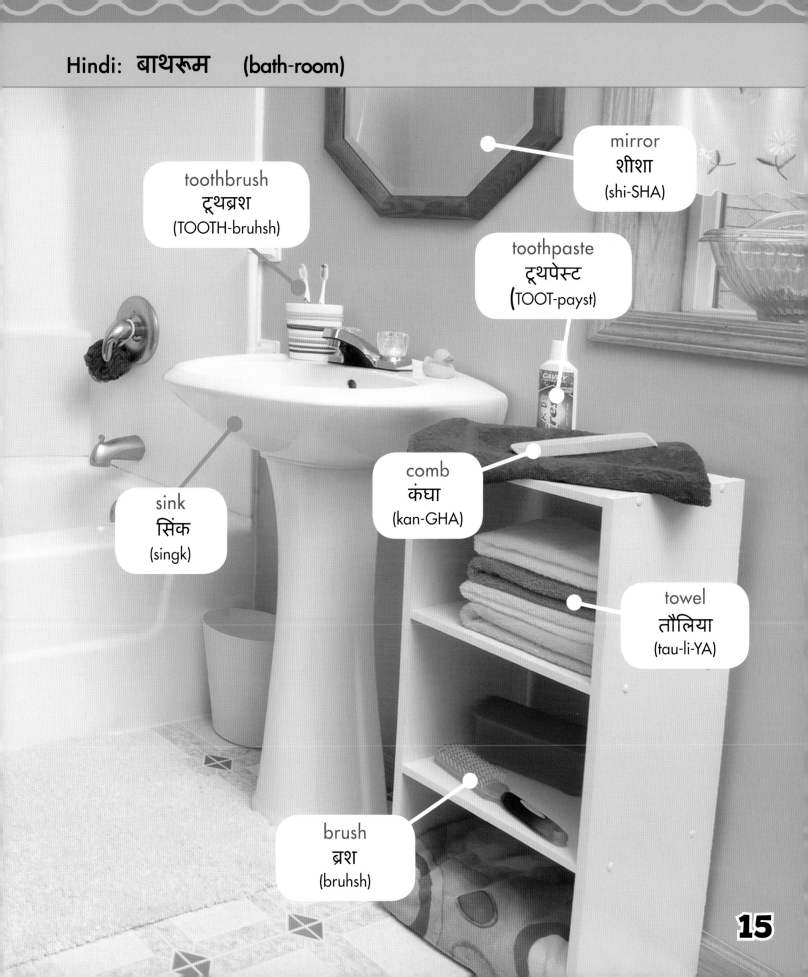

toothbrush
टूथब्रश
(TOOTH-bruhsh)

mirror
शीशा
(shi-SHA)

toothpaste
टूथपेस्ट
(TOOT-payst)

sink
सिंक
(singk)

comb
कंघा
(kan-GHA)

towel
तौलिया
(tau-li-YA)

brush
ब्रश
(bruhsh)

pot
बर्तन
(bar-tan)

hob
स्टोव
(stohv)

bowl
कटोरा
(ka-to-RA)

oven
चूल्हा
(chul-ha)

refrigerator
फ्रिज
(frij)

knife
चाकू
(CHA-koo)

table
मेज
(mez)

spoon
चम्मच
(cham-ma-ch)

plate
प्लेट
(playt)

fork
कांटा
(KAN-ta)

17

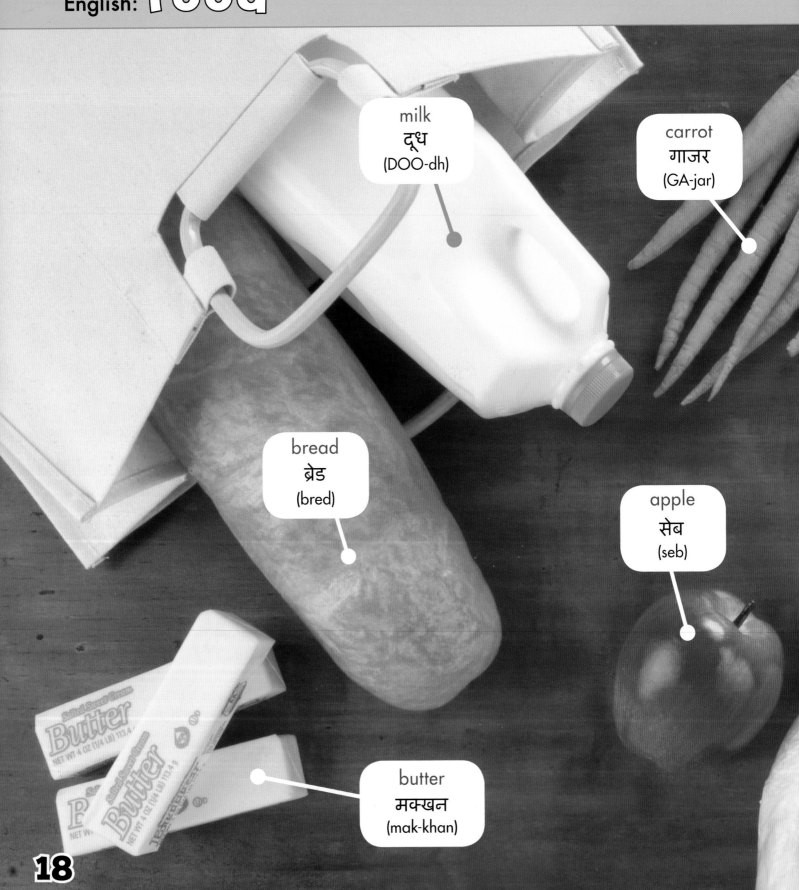

milk
दूध
(DOO-dh)

carrot
गाजर
(GA-jar)

bread
ब्रेड
(bred)

apple
सेब
(seb)

butter
मक्खन
(mak-khan)

18

egg
अंडा
(an-DA)

pea
मटर
(ma-tar)

orange
संतरा
(san-ta-RA)

sandwich
सैंडविच
(SAIND-witch)

rice
चावल
(CHA-val)

19

tractor
ट्रैक्टर
(traik-tar)

hay
भूसा
(bhoo-SA)

fence
बाड़ा
(ba-da)

farmer
किसान
(kis-AN)

pig
सूअर
(su-ar)

sheep
भेड़
(bhed)

horse
घोड़ा
(gho-DA)

barn
खलिहान
(kha-li-HAN)

cow
गाय
(gai)

chicken
मुर्गी
(mur-gee)

21

leaf
पत्ती
(pat-ti)

butterfly
तितली
(ti-ta-li)

flower
फूल
(phool)

trowel
बेलचा
(bel-CHA)

bird
पक्षी
(pak-shi)

worm
कीड़ा
(kee-DA)

plant
पौधा
(pau-DHA)

grass
घास
(ghaas)

Edamame Green Soybean
Tohya

$2.99
Net Weight
15 grams

80 days
Warm season
crop - plant after
last chance of
spring frost

So high in
protein, it is
called "the meat
without bones".
Boiled, beans
are popped out
of the pod into
your mouth for
a culinary
delight!

soil
धूल
(dhool)

seed
बीज
(beej)

23

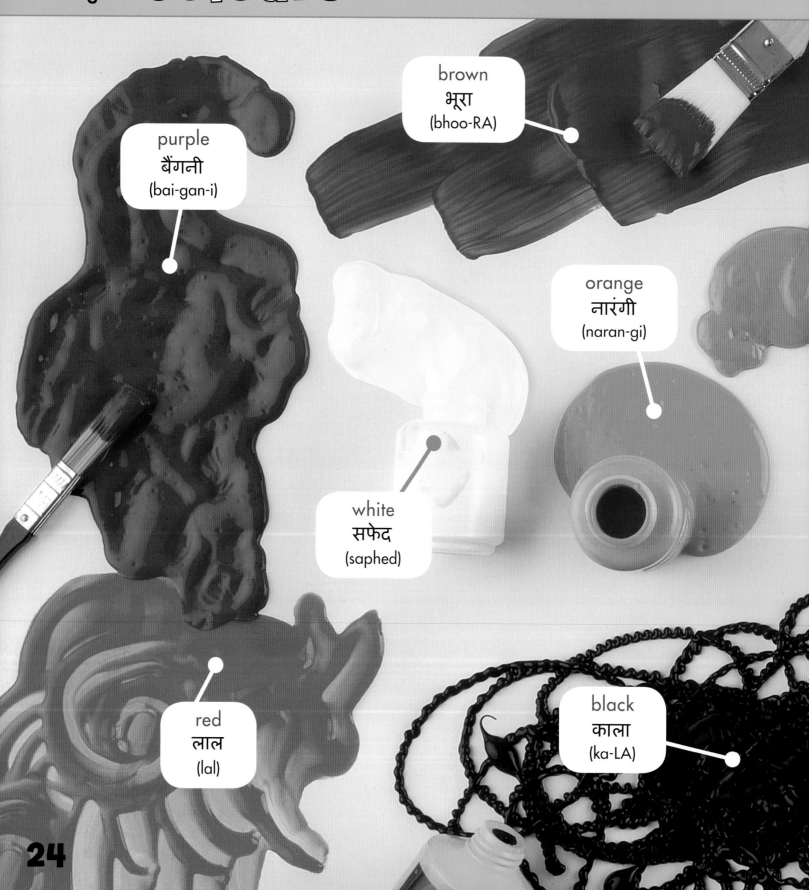

purple
बैंगनी
(bai-gan-i)

brown
भूरा
(bhoo-RA)

orange
नारंगी
(naran-gi)

white
सफेद
(saphed)

red
लाल
(lal)

black
काला
(ka-LA)

pink
गुलाबी
(gu-LA-bi)

blue
नीला
(nee-LA)

yellow
पीला
(pi-LA)

green
हरा
(ha-RA)

25

teacher
अध्यापिका
(ad-HYA-pika)

book
किताब
(ki-TAAB)

pencil
पेंसिल
(PEN-suhl)

crayon
क्रेयान
(cre-YAN)

desk
डेस्क
(desk)

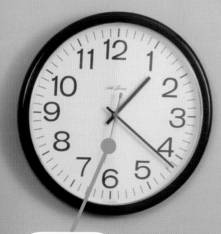

map
नक्शा
(nak-sha)

clock
घड़ी
(gha-rhi)

computer
कंप्यूटर
(kuhm-PYOO-tur)

chair
कुर्सी
(kur-si)

paper
कागज़
(KAA-guz)

27

traffic light
ट्रैफ़िक लाइट
(TREF-ik LITE)

library
पुस्तकालय
(pu-sta-KA-lay)

shop
स्टोर
(stor)

LIBRARY

ONE WAY

bicycle
साइकिल
(sai-kil)

car
कार
(kar)

tree
पेड़
(ped)

bus
बस
(BUHS)

park
पार्क
(par-k)

street
सड़क
(sa-dak)

sign
संकेत
(san-ket)

STOP

Numbers • संख्याएँ (sank-hy-ae)

1. one • एक (ek)
2. two • दो (do)
3. three • तीन (teen)
4. four • चार (char)
5. five • पाँच (panch)

6. six • छ: (chheh)
7. seven • सात (saat)
8. eight • आठ (art)
9. nine • नौ (nau)
10. ten • दस (das)

Useful phrases • उपयोगी वाक्यांश (upa-yo-gi vak-yan-sh)

yes • हाँ (HA)

no • नहीं (na-hi)

hello • नमस्ते (na-mas-tay)

goodbye • अलविदा (al-vi-DA)

good morning • शुभप्रभात (shu-bh pra-BHAA-t)

goodnight • शुभरात्रि (shu-bh-RA-tri)

please • कृपया (kri-pa-ya)

thank you • धन्यवाद (dhan-ya-VAD)

excuse me • क्षमा करें (ksha-MA ka-re)

My name is _____. • _____ मेरा नाम है. (mee-ra NAAM____hey)

Find out more

Look up more Hindi words in these books:

Hindi Children's Picture Dictionary (Hippocrene Books, 2006)

My First English-English-Hindi Dictionary. (HarperCollins, 2011)

Star Children's English-Hindi Picture Dictionary, Babita Varma (Star Books, 2010)

Websites

Visit these sites to learn more Hindi words:

http://www.indif.com/kids/learn_hindi/

http://www.akhlesh.com/

http://kidsone.in/hindi/learnhindi/hindi-letters.jsp

Raintree is an imprint of Capstone Global Library Limited, a company incorporated in England and Wales having its registered office at 7 Pilgrim Street, London, EC4V 6LB – Registered company number: 6695582

www.raintree.co.uk
myorders@raintree.co.uk

Text © Capstone Global Library Limited 2015
First published in hardback in 2015
Paperback edition first published in 2016
The moral rights of the proprietor have been asserted.

Designed by Lori Bye
Picture research by Wanda Winch
Production by Eric Manske
Originated by Capstone Global Library Ltd
Printed and bound in China

ISBN 978 1 474 70687 2 (hardback)
19 18 17 16
10 9 8 7 6 5 4 3 2 1

ISBN 978 1 474 70693 3 (paperback)
20 19 18 17 16
10 9 8 7 6 5 4 3 2 1

British Library Cataloguing in Publication Data
A full catalogue record for this book is available from the British Library.

Acknowledgements
We would like to thank the following for permission to reproduce photographs: Capstone Studio/Gary Sundermeyer, 20 (farmer with tractor, pig); Capstone Studio/Karon Dubke, cover (ball, sock), 1, 3, 4-5, 6-7, 8-9, 10-11, 12-13, 14-15, 16-17, 18-19, 22-23, 24-25, 26-27; Image Farm, back cover, 1, 2, 31, 32 (design elements); iStockphoto/Andrew Gentry, 28 (main street); Photodisc, cover (flower); Shutterstock/Adrian Matthiassen, cover (butterfly); David Hughes, 20 (hay); Eric Isselee, cover (horse), 20-21 (horse); hamurishi, 28 (bike); Ievgeniia Tikhonova, 21 (chickens); Jim Mills, 29 (stop sign); Kelli Westfal, 28 (traffic light); Margo Harrison, 20 (sheep); MaxPhoto, 21 (cow and calf); Melinda Fawver, 29 (bus); Robert Elias, 20-21 (barn, fence); Vladimir Mucibabic, 28-29 (city skyline).

Every effort has been made to contact copyright holders of material reproduced in this book. Any omissions will be rectified in subsequent printings if notice is given to the publisher.

Note to parents, teachers and librarians
Learning to speak a second language at a young age has been shown to improve overall academic performance, boost problem-solving ability and foster an appreciation for other cultures. Early exposure to language skills provides a strong foundation for other subject areas, including maths and reasoning. Introducing children to a second language can help to lay the groundwork for future academic success and cultural awareness.